THE

IMMATURE
BOOK CLUB

Self published, London, England
First printed January 2014
Copyright ©2014 The Immature Book Club
All rights reserved

"Dear Poo-poohead" by The Immature Book Club
ISBN-13: 978-1494819682 I ISBN-10:1494819686

Author's Note
This book is not to be taken seriously. However the characters, places and incidents either are the products of our imagination or are used fictitiously, and any resemblance to actual persons, living or dead, events, or locales is entirely coincidental.

CONTENTS

DEAR POO-POOHEAD,

WE HOPE YOU ENJOY THIS WASTE OF SPACE BOOK.

IT PROBABLY HAS BEEN GIVEN TO YOU AS A PRANK OR AS

SOMETHING TO ENTERTAIN YOU WHILST DOING YOUR NO. 2!

EITHER WAY, THIS BOOK IS GOING TO BRING YOU EITHER

JOY OR UTTER DISGUST.

———

THE IMMATURE BOOK CLUB

@IMMATUREBC

#DEARPOOPOOHEAD

HOW TO SPOT A POO-POOHEAD

ALWAYS ON THE TOILET.

IT'S ALMOST LIKE THEIR OFFICE.

LOVES A GOOD TOILET CONVERSATION

HAVE A NICKNAME FOR THE TOILET

"THE POOP MACHINE!"

2

THE PERFECT POO

LET'S SET THE SCENE...

MAKE SURE YOU HAVE A NICE CLEAN TOILET.

THE ROOM MUST BE AT A GOOD MILD TEMPERATURE.

IF NOT, CONSIDER TURNING THE HEATING ON.

REMEMBER TO CRACK OPEN A WINDOW.

MAKE SURE IT'S IN THE EARLY MORNING (WITHOUT ANY
CLOTHES ON TO AVOID SMELLY CLOTHES) OR LATE AT
NIGHT AFTER YOUR LONG DAY TO WIND-DOWN
(AGAIN NO CLOTHES).

THE BEST POO SESSIONS ARE ENJOYED

IN THE NUDE.

PLACE A LITTLE TISSUE INSIDE THE TOILET BOWL
TO AVOID SPLASHING.

PUT SOME BACKGROUND MUSIC ON,
READ A NEWSPAPER, MAGAZINE OR HAVE YOUR TABLET
AT HAND TO KEEP YOU OCCUPIED.
THE TOILET IS THE BEST PLACE TO THINK!

WE STRONGLY SUGGEST YOU POO WITH THE ODD FLUSH IN
BETWEEN TO AVOID THE AROMA GETTING OUT OF HAND.

NOW YOU'RE READY TO ENJOY YOUR POO SESSION!

3

POO-POO TALES

MY DATE YESTERDAY WAS AH-MAZING!

I SHOULDN'T HAVE ORDERED THAT CURRY THOUGH.

MY STOMACH'S BEEN RUMBLING ALL DAY.

2 HOURS LATER...

OH MY GOSH! I'M AN HOUR AWAY FROM HOME AND IT

FEELS LIKE I'M GOING TO POOP MYSELF <u>NOW!</u>

WHY CAN'T THIS BUS HURRY UP?!

SHOULD I GET OFF AT THE NEXT STOP?

OH NO! I NEED TO GO...

I'M SO TIRED, I NEED SOME CAFFEINE.
TO DRINK OR NOT TO DRINK? NOW THAT'S THE QUESTION.

4 HOURS LATER...

I SHOULDN'T HAVE DRANK THAT COFFEE!
I'VE BEEN POOING ALL DAY!

I REALLY NEED TO GO, BUT I DON'T WANT TO GO HERE!
LAST WEEK, TANYA WAS CAUGHT POOING IN THE SCHOOL
TOILETS AND OUT OF PURE FEAR SHE RUSHED OUT WITH
POO ON THE BOTTOM OF HER SKIRT!
SHE HASN'T BEEN BACK EVER SINCE.
OK, I'M GOING IN...

40 MINUTES LATER...

CRAP! I NEED TO GET OUT OF HERE. THE WOMEN OUTSIDE
OF THE CUBICLES ARE STARTING TO ASK QUESTIONS:
"SHE'S BEEN IN THERE FOR A WHILE NOW...
I WONDER WHO IT IS?"
"SHOULD WE WAIT TO SEE HER FACE? LET'S WAIT."
"SHE'S BEEN IN THERE FOR AT LEAST 20 MINUTES!"
MY BREAK IS NEARLY FINISHED.
YES! THEY'RE LEAVING!
THANK GOD THEY DIDN'T WAIT. I WOULD HAVE HAD TO
STAY IN HERE UNTIL THEY DID!

4

THINGS THAT MAKE YOU GO POO

BANANAS

PINEAPPLES

PRUNES

PEARS

FIGS

PEACHES

BEANS

BROCCOLI

FLAXSEEDS

CARROTS

OATMEAL

WHOLE GRAINS

BRAN CEREAL

MINTS

FRESHLY BAKED CAKES & BREADS

COFFEE

SPICY CURRY (FOR MOST PEOPLE)

5

POO CONVERSATION STARTERS

"I LOVE INDIAN FOOD
BUT IT JUST GOES RIGHT THROUGH ME!"

"DID YOU KNOW THAT MINTS HAVE
LAXATIVE PROPERTIES?"

"DO PROTEIN SHAKES GIVE YOU THE RUNS TOO?"

6

POO METHODS

SOME SQUAT.

BE PREPARED TO DIG!

YOU ARE RECOMMENDED TO DIG A HOLE 6-8 INCHES DEEP.

NO POOPING ON THE SURFACE PLEASE.

NO TOILET PAPER?

IN SOME COUNTRIES AFTER A POO, THEY CLEAN THEIR
BACKSIDE USING THEIR LEFT HAND AND
A JUG FULL OF WATER.
THIS IS USUALLY DONE IN MUSLIM COUNTRIES AND
THEREFORE EXPLAINS WHY SOME PEOPLE DON'T USE THEIR
LEFT HAND FOR EATING OR HAND-SHAKING.

THE USUAL.

A TOILET AND TOILET PAPER.

IF USING A PUBLIC TOILET,

WE SUGGEST THAT YOU PLACE TOILET PAPER AROUND THE

SEAT TO AVOID CATCHING ANYTHING.

POO-POO
NOTES
AND DOODLES

(JUST IN CASE YOU'RE STILL AT IT AFTER READING)

....
....
....
....
....
....
....
....
....
....
....
....
....

38169101R00026

Printed in Great Britain
by Amazon